ALSO BY KATHRYN REED

Sleeping with Strangers:
An Airbnb Host's Life in Lake Tahoe and Mexico

Lake Tahoe Trails For All Seasons:
Must-Do Hiking and Snowshoe Treks

The Dirt Around Lake Tahoe: Must-Do Scenic Hikes

Snowshoeing Around Lake Tahoe
MUST-DO SCENIC TREKS

KATHRYN REED

Snowshoeing Around Lake Tahoe: Must-Do Scenic Treks
by Kathryn Reed. Published by Kathryn Reed
P.O. Box 853, Chico, CA 95927
www.KathrynReed.com
© 2020 Kathryn Reed.
All rights reserved. No part of this book may be reproduced or transmitted in any form or by any means, electronic, mechanical, photocopying, recording, or otherwise, without prior written permission. For permissions contact:
kr@kathrynreed.com
Library of Congress Control Number: 2020900179
ISBN: 978-1-952003-00-4
Front and back cover, and interior photos © Kathryn Reed.
Author photo © Susan Wood.
Cover design by Ponderosa Pine Design.

Contents

South Shore/American River Canyon
Roundabout at Heavenly 2
Becker Peak 5
Emerald Bay 8
Fallen Leaf Lake 10
Tallac Site 12
Baldwin Beach 14
Maggie's Peak 16
Van Sickle Bi-State Park 18
Angora Ridge 21
Echo Lake Ridge 24
Twin Peaks 26
Emerald Bay Campground 28
High Meadow 30
Grass Lake 32
Lake Tahoe Golf Course 35

West Shore
Sugar Pine Point 38

East Shore
Marlette Lake 42
Skunk Harbor 45

Alpine County
Elephants Back 48
Carson Pass 51
Hope Valley 54

Acknowledgments

I have always found snowshoeing to be more enjoyable with friends. Thank you to all my winter sports partners for breaking trail with me.

It was my parents who first introduced me to the outdoors in various forms – camping, water skiing, hiking, snow skiing. I will always be grateful. My mom became a snowshoer after I moved to Lake Tahoe, making many outings even more special.

Sue Wood, Rosemary Manning and Donna Rockwood were on many of these excursions. They helped rate the treks in terms of scenic quality and challenge.

Thank you to Christel Hall for editing the book and to Vicky Shea for the cover design. Joann Eisenbrandt was patient with getting this into print. Several people offered advice with the title, for which I am grateful.

A big thank you to all the supporters of *Lake Tahoe News*, who for nine years were part of my daily life in some form and who first inspired me to write these stories.

Introduction

Enjoying the outdoors is a big part of what Lake Tahoe is all about. Tahoe has something for everyone. It can mean watching the snow fall while staying warm by the fire or being an Olympic gold medalist. This book is for all those athletes in between.

These snowshoe treks were originally written for *Lake Tahoe News (LTN)*. LakeTahoeNews.net was the preeminent news source from 2009-2018. They were all written by me, an average athlete. The stories have been revised to make sense for readers who live in or outside the Lake Tahoe Basin.

Many of the excursions can be done on snowshoes or cross country skis. It will depend on your ability level. I say if you can walk, you can snowshoe. Your gait is just a little wider. The bonus about snowshoeing is that it's free; no need to pay to play at a resort – though that is possible. It's good exercise, but more important it's an opportunity to get into nature, to be immersed in her beauty, and to venture places not everyone has gone.

Four people provided input on the challenge and scenic ratings in the book. These were not included with the original *LTN* stories.

Snow conditions will be a factor in considering the challenge. There is a big difference between breaking trail and someone having beaten you to it.

Another added challenge will be the elevation; the starting point as well as the maximum level you will hit. Living at sea level may make some excursions seem harder.

Be smart when you play outside. Take more water than you think you will need. It's easy to become dehydrated in winter because the temperature and less sweating may make you forget to drink. Take extra clothing, food and a first aid kit. Whatever you pack in, be sure to pack out. Don't expect your cell phone to work in the wilderness. It can be a good idea to let someone know when you should return so help can be summoned if you are overdue.

Know if dogs are allowed, and if you need water for them or if enough will be supplied by streams and lakes. Some may be frozen in winter, and not all dogs eat snow. Plowing through powder will be more exhausting for a dog. Short-haired dogs may need a coat. At various times be sure to check their paws for snow accumulation.

Take pictures, but leave everything else as you found it. Now, go put on those snowshoes.

Kathryn Reed

South Shore/ American River Canyon

Snowshoeing to Emerald Bay when Highway 89 is closed is not possible every winter.

Roundabout: Not A Green Run Going Uphill

Scenic: 8
Challenge: 7
Special note: Don't go when there are skiers.
Getting there: From South Lake Tahoe, turn onto Ski Run Boulevard. Turn left on Needle Peak Road, right on Wildwood Avenue, left on Saddle Road, right on Keller Road, and right on Sherman Way. The road dead-ends at Sherman. There is a gate there. Start walking.

Solitude. Blue. Calm. Incredible. Inspirational. Awe. These are just a few of the words that came to mind while looking at Lake Tahoe from the top of Gunbarrel at Heavenly Mountain Resort.

It's a limited window when one can snowshoe this route. It must be before the ski season opens or after it ends. It is an impossible snowshoe during the ski season; too many people are on skis on what seems like a narrow path. On snowshoes, it's like being on a road – wide, with plenty of room.

Roundabout lives up to its name. The circuitous route is usually the easy way down the mountain to California Lodge. Going up on snowshoes, ascending

Maggie's Peak: Views All Along The Way

Scenic: 6
Challenge: 7
Special note: Go early because parking can be an issue.
Getting there: From South Lake Tahoe, go north on Highway 89. Park at the Bayview Campground on the left. This is before the parking lot for Vikingsholm. Walk through the campground. There will be a sign indicating left for Cascade Falls, right for Desolation Wilderness. Go right.

Maggie's cleavage took our breath away.

That's what we called the saddle of Maggie's Peak because, well, these two peaks in Desolation Wilderness are named for a woman who was well endowed. That strip of land in between the peaks has some outstanding views.

Desolation Wilderness appears to go on forever. So expansive it seems a bit foreboding, even though we were immersed in it for nearly the entire snowshoe. No wonder Eagle Lake is chilly in the summer; it's often frozen in the winter. On this particular day Emerald Bay could have been renamed Sapphire Bay because of the rich, deep blue hue that spilled forth.

about 1,600 feet to an elevation of more than 8,200 feet, cannot be described as easy. The beauty, though, takes one's breath away; or maybe that's due to the climb or the altitude.

While it isn't necessary to have poles, it would be a good idea for anyone with knee or balance issues.

Other than the crunching of the snowshoes against the terrain there was silence. Be sure to pause to hear the stillness and appreciate the beauty that seems to change at every corner. Various views of Lake Tahoe spill forth. Mount Tallac and Pyramid Peak stand out at various times. The casinos, while dominant in some ways, seem so insignificant from this vantage point.

The pinnacle is the top of Gunbarrel and the ski resort's tram. This is one view that never gets old. The whole lake unfolds in a breathtaking view that seems almost surreal.

Instead of going back the same way, it was time to see what it's like to snowshoe The Face. A zigzag approach seemed best so as not to tumble and become a snowball that careens to the bottom. It took some patience and focus because some rocks weren't far beneath the snow.

At times the snow was powdery, making the snowshoes a much-needed tool. Too bad the poles were in the garage. Other spots were crusty, making the trek more of a challenge. Instead of going all the way down this route, just like on skis, it's possible to hook up with Roundabout to make it out on a less steep grade.

To do a round trip on Roundabout and skip The Face is just more than 5 miles.

SOUTH SHORE/AMERICAN RIVER CANYON

Becker Peak: Summit Is Worth The Effort

Scenic: 8
Challenge: 6
Special note: A sno-park pass is required from Nov. 1-May 30. They are available online.
Getting there: From South Lake Tahoe, take Highway 50 west over Echo Summit. Turn right on Johnson Pass Road. Parking is to the right.

Crevasses and the refraction of light had Echo Lake looking like it mirrored a sky filled with puffy cumulus clouds. It was as though a pale blue marker had been used to draw circles on the white sheet of ice.

From our vantage point atop Becker Peak and then walking along the ridge, Echo Lake was mesmerizing. Nine of us spent a morning snowshoeing to the top of Becker Peak – elevation 8,391 feet.

Snowshoeing in drought years requires seeking out higher elevations because it's only dirt at lake level. This is one route that should be good no matter what it looks like at lake level in the winter. While some of us were in shorts and others in short sleeves on this warm spring day, the snowshoes were definitely needed. Snow even covered the road leading to Echo Lake.

A late morning start was ideal so the snow had some give to it. Almost everyone used poles, which was good on the steeper sections for the ascent and decline. The worst part, at least in terms of exertion, is turning off the road and heading straight up to the ridge. We made the left directly across from the Berkeley Camp and by a few no parking signs.

Some in the group advised that it's better to start a little farther up the road during hiking season to avoid what is bushy terrain without snow.

If the route up does not take your breath away, the views on top of the ridge are bound to. Flagpole, Angora Peak, Dicks Peak, the back of Mount Tallac, Jakes Peak, the Angora burn area and Lake Tahoe all spill forth in an array of winter beauty. While it would be possible to call it a day at this point in terms of scenic beauty, the views only get better.

Even though Craig, a snowshoer in our party, was correct to say the hard part was over, there was still some climbing to do. I was glad to be with people who had done this trek before. Even though other snowshoers had laid down a trail before us, their route was a bit sketchy at times. Some said there was no way to get lost, but I also believe there is a first for everything.

Not too much farther and we saw the slopes of Sierra-at-Tahoe on our left and a frozen Echo Lake to our right. We got to what could be another stopping point where there was an incredible expansive view of Echo Lake. We paused long enough for photos before making the final ascent to Becker Peak.

The peak itself is a pile of large rocks. Off came the snowshoes so we could scramble to the top. Even AJ the dog was able to make it up to the top. We sat there a bit, having a bite to eat, taking in the views and putting layers back on to ward off the nippy wind. It was 360 degrees of pure Sierra serenity.

Skiers were along the edge of Echo Lake. Talking Mountain, from this vantage point, looks like it would be easy to reach. We climbed about 1,000 feet to get to this point. It's about 4.5 miles round trip. We chose a lower route back that provided more views of Echo Lake and Lake Tahoe.

Emerald Bay: Without Vehicle Traffic

Scenic: 8
Challenge: 3
Special note: This snowshoe trek is not available every winter. Caltrans will have road closure information.
Getting there: From South Lake Tahoe, go north on Highway 89. There will be a gate across the highway; park where you can.

Cascade Lake looked like it needed a Zamboni machine to clear off the snow to make it a perfect skating rink. Emerald Bay was eerily black, as though perhaps some creature of the lake lurked below. Tahoe Tessie?

It was one of those rare winter opportunities when Highway 89 was closed to vehicles and open to foot traffic. Parking at the gate near the entrance to Eagle Point Campground, we strapped on snowshoes to make the 1.1-mile trek to appropriately named Inspiration Point.

Fortunately, someone beat us there so we didn't have to break trail. Only one path heads up the road – wide enough for snowshoes, but a definite single file approach. Meandering up the hairpin turns, going slower than the 10 mph limit, we came to one of the most scenic areas in the Lake Tahoe Basin. The private Cascade Lake is to our left, Emerald Bay on our right, and behind us Lake Tahoe. Cascade looked frozen – as if a hockey game or figure skating competition should be under way.

As the M.S. Dixie II paddle-wheeler churned into Emerald Bay, the normal blue water looked foreboding. Ice lingered on the edge near Vikingsholm castle, signaling just how cold the water was. Fannette Island was dusted in snow from a recent storm, making the teahouse look almost like a gingerbread house sprinkled with powder sugar.

The snow was light, the air cool. Traipsing up we were warmed by the sun, but as soon as we paused at the lookout area, we were chilled in the shade. We didn't linger long, having many times before read the informative interpretive signs explaining what we were looking at and how glaciers formed these bodies of water. They are worth reading for first-timers or to get a refresher about the area's history.

Heading back, it was as though we were surrounded by water now that Lake Tahoe was in front of us. It was truly magical, especially because this isn't something one can do every day or even every winter. Highway 89 closes throughout the winter because of avalanche conditions and heavy snowfall, so it's hit or miss when this snowshoe route is an option.

Fallen Leaf Lake: A Wintertime Wonder

Scenic: 7
Challenge: 3
Special note: A sno-park permit is required. The permits may be bought online.
Getting there: From South Lake Tahoe, head north on Highway 89. Go through Camp Richardson. Pass the turn for Fallen Leaf Lake. Cathedral Road is on the left.

Strapping on our snowshoes in the Cathedral Road parking lot off Highway 89 we began our journey into the wild. At least it seemed that way as the quiet enveloped us.

The snow-covered road was wide enough to stride along in pairs and not be knocked over by one of our four-legged friends. At times the trail narrowed from the thick conifers, then suddenly it was as though there was a meadow of snow.

Not far in we veered to the left to take the trail instead of staying on the road even though no motor vehicles can drive on it with snow on the ground. It became single track. One by one we sauntered forward. At times water crossed our path, necessitating a bit of improvising. This can happen in the early and late seasons depending on the snowfall accumulations and the subsequent melt.

Taylor Creek was flowing toward Lake Tahoe at what looked like capacity and it wasn't even spring yet.

Onward we went, heading to Fallen Leaf Lake to the left instead of going right which would have us loop back to the parking lot. Up and over the dam with snowshoes on takes a bit of dexterity and concentration.

Contrails lined the blue sky, crossing through the wispy clouds to create a one-of-a-kind canvas. The still water reflected the mountains of Desolation Wilderness until the canines sent ripples across the alpine lake.

Break time meant peeling off clothes as the sun beat down on us. Most of the dogs ventured into Fallen Leaf Lake to retrieve sticks, unfazed by the ice floating nearby.

Back we went, though not exactly as we had come. We ended up making a loop to our left, through what during late summer is one of the most incredible patches of lupine. On this day it was the stark white bark of the aspen grove that captured our attention.

From the parking lot to the dam is about 1 mile. It's possible to spend all day in this area exploring.

Tallac Site: Window To The South Shore's Past

Scenic: 7
Challenge: 2
Special note: Good for all ages.
Getting there: From South Lake Tahoe, go north on Highway 89 toward Emerald Bay. At Camp Richardson, turn right at the lodge. Drive down to the parking lot at the Grove restaurant. Tallac Site is to the left.

Apparently for rich San Franciscans, Lake Tahoe's winters were too harsh. Instead of embracing the elements and the beauty, they boarded up their homes, packed their belongings and went to the flat land for most of the year. Of course, those who summered on the shores of Lake Tahoe in the first half of the 20th century didn't have all the modern conveniences we have today.

Had those with last names like Pope, Baldwin and Heller decided to reside year-round at what is now known as the Tallac Historic Site, it's possible the winter experience would be much different. Maybe it would still be privately owned and off-limits to the rest of us.

Today, it is so incredibly tranquil. Few people venture to this part of the South Shore in winter. It's almost like a ghost town. Sure, the buildings there are closed up just like when the area was privately owned. But there is still plenty to see. The U.S. Forest Service has done a great job putting up signs telling about the history of this site.

Nineteen buildings are dispersed on what were three estates. (Most are open in the summer.) The 74 acres are listed on the National Register of Historic Places. Restoration work continues on the buildings and grounds.

Imagine what it would have been like a century ago to live here. Imagine the summers back then compared to today. Same lake, same trees, same beach – but a different time makes for a different world. This trek is a bit present day, a bit yesteryear.

It's possible to end up at Baldwin Beach. Going along the beach back to the parking lot is an option instead of returning through the Tallac Site. Routes make it so it can be a loop or an out-and-back. This also means the mileage can vary. Plan on it being close to 3 miles round trip. This trek is good on snowshoes, cross country skis and snow boots.

Baldwin Beach: A Shoreline Jaunt

Scenic: 7
Challenge: 2
Special note: Pay attention to the no parking signs along the highway to avoid being towed.
Getting there: From South Lake Tahoe, go north on Highway 89. Park at the gate for Baldwin Beach where it says "Recreation Area Closed for the Season." If you reach Cascade Properties, you went too far.

The few feet of sand next to the lake may have one thinking a towel and book would be good things to bring next time. This happens on winter days that feel more like spring. The snow had softened enough by late morning to have a little give and made walking pleasurable. Lake Tahoe was like glass, beckoning anyone foolish enough to come play with her. But we knew better. She is no friend this time of year – this icy bowl of water.

Outdoor enthusiasts had laid several tracks. An etiquette reminder: if possible, don't walk in the tracks of cross country skiers. Even though dogs are not allowed, people have left behind evidence their pets were there.

SOUTH SHORE/AMERICAN RIVER CANYON

Meandering down what looks like a forested tunnel due to thick conifers on either side had altered my state of mind. I'm lost in this wonderland. Inhaling, exhaling. Oh, that mountain air. Less than a mile in, the terrain opened, and Lake Tahoe's deep blue waters were just steps away. We headed north along the beach. Mount Tallac was to our left covered with snow.

No one was in sight, yet the tracks proved plenty of people had beaten us to this little slice of Tahoe splendor. We went as far as we could. A creek prevented us from crossing. Although the water level was low, there would be no way not to get our feet wet. No matter the outside temperature, wet feet can lead to frostbite. At times this inlet can be crossed on the ice. However, crossing any ice in Tahoe is tricky because of the freeze-thaw factor. It's not always as solid as one might think it is. When the area is crossable, it becomes a bit of an architectural tour with all the shoreline homes.

We turned around and headed toward Taylor Creek. A large predator bird was circling in the distance – perhaps a hawk of some sort. It's one of those incredibly easy outings, whether on snowshoes or cross country skis, because it's all flat. No chance of getting lost with the lake on one side. It is one of the most scenic places to visit – even more so in the winter than summer.

SOUTH SHORE/AMERICAN RIVER CANYON

Snowshoeing to Granite Lake was pretty, while the final push to the saddle of Maggie's Peak was spectacular. Granite Lake was our original destination. Getting there was more of a vertical ascent than a leisurely switchback. This was not a trek on which to set speed records, so Donna, Rosemary, Sue and I – and dogs AJ and Cody – stopped several times along the way.

The path was well worn with plenty of snowshoers having been there before us. It's single track. At times all we could hear was the crunching of the snow beneath the claws strapped to our boots.

Large boulders near Granite Lake and protruding from the ice provided a lunch spot. Plenty of tracks across the frozen mass proved the ice was thick. Not a cloud could be seen. It was one of those idyllic Tahoe blue skies. One of Maggie's Peaks rose from the far end of the lake.

Donna and Sue perused the map, figuring out the cleavage wasn't that much farther, so we carried on. The trailhead is at 6,890 feet. Granite Lake is at 7,700 feet and the saddle is at 8,330 feet. It's about 1½ miles to the lake and another eight-tenths of a mile to the saddle. While there had been wonderful views along the way, the best were definitely at the saddle.

Van Sickle Park: The Country's Only Bi-State Park

Scenic: 6
Challenge: 5
Special note: Free parking is difficult to find. Casino valet may be an option.
Getting there: From the South Shore, turn on Heavenly Village Way. This dead ends at the park. Paid parking is available at a garage on Bellamy Court, which is off Heavenly Village Way.

Everything changes with a little snow. Some things even get better, like the views from Van Sickle Bi-State Park.

While we were familiar with the trail, we were thankful others had gone before us to ensure we were going in the correct direction. This 725-acre park on the South Shore provides stunning views of Lake Tahoe by snowshoeing just a short distance. The scenic outlook is a mere 0.4 miles from the trailhead.

One problem in winter is the required walking to get to the trailhead. The California Tahoe Conservancy and Nevada Division of State Lands, which own and operate the park, shut the entrance gate from Nov. 1-April 30. With nearby casinos eliminating free parking, parking can be a bit of a conundrum.

SOUTH SHORE/AMERICAN RIVER CANYON

There is a distinct trail almost directly across from Harrah's casino's back parking lot. Warning: it can be a bit precarious to cross the street without a crosswalk.

We sauntered up a little hill and then went left on South Tahoe Public Utility District's road before we took a left onto the park's road. A trail sign clearly indicates where the path really begins. It's also possible to start at the gate to the park at the intersection of Montreal Road and Heavenly Village Parkway.

With part of the actual path a bit icy, it was great to have the claws of snowshoes to dig into the terrain. However, patches of dirt had to be walked on, too. Conditions will depend on the time of year and the amount of snow that winter.

Climbing to the vista is well worth the views of Lake Tahoe and the mountain peaks. The Stateline casinos, Rabe Meadow and Round Hill stand out as well.

Tracks from other snowshoers, hikers and cross country skiers were evident. Even super wide bike tires had left their mark in the snow. It's a great place for dogs, too.

Signs tell people about the terrain as well as where to go. The Gondola Fire of 2002 is talked about because many of the charred trees remain in the park. The story of sugar pine plantings is also posted.

We took the upper turnoff for the Cal/Neva Loop. It heads toward California, with a spur going to the Saddle Road neighborhood. It was quiet, even secluded. At one point the pines gave us a sense of being enclosed in some far-off winter wonderland. The snow was softer, powder-like. Fewer people had been there. Lake Tahoe was glassy and inviting, if only it weren't so darn cold.

Starting after noon meant the temps were warmer and the afternoon light provided colors and contrasts different than those cast by Mother Nature in the morning. Soon we were reminded how close to civilization we were as the Heavenly Mountain Resort gondola whirred above us.

We took the Barn Trail, knowing it would lead us to the main park road that would drop us off near the park's entrance. With the abundance of trails, mileage is going to vary. Check out this link to get a map with distances: http://parks.nv.gov/forms/VanSickle_Bi_State_Park_Map.pdf.

SOUTH SHORE/AMERICAN RIVER CANYON

Angora Ridge: Views In Multiple Directions

Scenic: 6
Challenge: 5
Special note: Parking is a problem.
Getting there: From South Lake Tahoe, at the Y go straight on Lake Tahoe Boulevard toward South Tahoe High School or the Angora burn area. Turn right on Tahoe Mountain Road. Go right at the T intersection. Go left at the next T. The road curves a bit. Go slow. Parking in front of the gate at the start of the trail is the best bet to avoid being towed.

The trek to Angora Ridge, like most routes going uphill, is all about the conditions. When it's slick, it's about having good claws to grab the hard pack snow. Breaking trail is a workout. It's a climb, no doubt about that. But the views – oh, they're worth it.

The 1.8 miles can feel a bit longer than that, which could be because the ridge is a thousand feet higher than lake level. It was five of us and a dog on this day, heading to the lookout at an elevation of 7,256 feet. The start was deceiving because of how flat it was – meadow-like, really. With this being a road, it is wide enough to walk side by side.

The others were in front of us chattering away; their loss because mom and I were sure an eagle, with its distinctive wingspan and white markings, flew overhead. Bald eagles are common in this part of Tahoe.

Up we went in almost a straight path. No switchbacks to contend with. Mount Tallac was visible to our right through the looming conifers. Gradually some charred trees come into sight to our left, remnants of the 2007 Angora Fire that burned about 3,100 acres, mostly U.S. Forest Service land. It was this federal property that we were on. From the ridge, the Angora burn area was unmistakable. New houses prove the resilience of the 254 homeowners who lost their homes. Many of the matchstick-like trees still stand.

The old fire lookout remains on top of Angora Ridge. A Forest Service forester built it in 1924. It was converted into a residence for Civilian Conservation Corps members, who in 1935 built a larger lookout nearby. No longer is this an active fire lookout. However, the buildings are eligible for inclusion on the National Register of Historic Places.

Looking north is Fallen Leaf Lake, with the base of Mount Tallac seeming to touch the far shore.

Up another mile is the parking lot for Angora Lakes Resort, with its two lakes. During the summer, the eight cabins are available for rent. Dogs must be leashed and are not allowed in the lakes. Opened in the 1920s, the resort is so popular that it's usually booked a year in advance.

This trek is doable for experienced cross country skiers. It is more difficult on skis than snowshoes because of the climb and descent.

Echo Lake Ridge: Full Of Beauty

Scenic: 6
Challenge: 4
Special note: A sno-park pass is required from Nov. 1-May 30. They are available online.
Getting there: From South Lake Tahoe, go west on Highway 50 to the top of Echo Summit. Turn right on Johnson Pass Road. Follow the road to the sno-park area. Cross the road and begin the trek on the road to Echo Lake.

A short jaunt up to the ridge above Echo Lake was a much-needed reminder of just how gorgeous this area is. Sometimes it's easy to take the beauty of the greater Lake Tahoe area for granted when one is immersed in daily life.

Stripped down to short sleeves – two of the five on the outing were in shorts – it was a glorious spring day. Not a cloud was in the sky. A cool breeze greeted us as we hiked farther on the ridge.

It's amazing how in less than 1½ miles we had a spectacular view of what seemed like the entire Tahoe basin. Mostly, though, it was the South Shore that spilled forth. At that elevation it was a good reminder of how this really is a forest and not a concrete jungle.

SOUTH SHORE/AMERICAN RIVER CANYON

On this particular day the road to Echo Lake was wide, matted down and easy to walk without snowshoes. Two in our group had been there just a couple weeks before when it was a different world because of the fresh snow. Then the snow was a couple feet deep, making it much more of a workout. That's the thing about playing in the snow; conditions will vary.

We passed by the frozen lake, crossed the dam and headed up to get to the point where we'd get that view. Others, though, had stopped to play on the frozen Lower Echo Lake – cross country skiing and skate skiing. Once across the dam we all had our snowshoes on.

We opted to head toward Flagpole Peak (elevation 8,363 feet). At one point we turned around to look down on some of the devices used for avalanche control above Highway 50.

It's the 360-degree views that make this such a great jaunt. It's relatively easy, and at just less than 3½ miles round trip, it should be done every year. Besides seeing Lake Tahoe in the distance, there are iconic peaks like Freel and Becker scratching the sky.

Twin Peaks: Short Scamper, Big Views

Scenic: 6
Challenge: 4
Special note: Good for most ages.
Getting there: From the Y in South Lake Tahoe, continue on Lake Tahoe Boulevard. Turn left on Sawmill Road. Park immediately in the lot to the left.

Easy, fun, scenic. Scampering up Twin Peaks on snowshoes encompasses all of these elements.

It's one of those jaunts that is great on a day when you want a little exercise outdoors, but don't have a ton of time. Of course, snow conditions always play a role in how long an excursion will take. It's also one of those sojourns where, if it's a warm day, it's worth lingering a bit. The views are some of the best for so little effort. The top provides an ideal lunch spot and place to sit with a book, or to just meditate a while, remembering why Lake Tahoe is so special.

Beneath us the snow was firm. It was nice to have the claws on the shoes so we didn't slip. Although the route is not extremely steep, it is definitely uphill without any plateaus to change the pitch. This is a fun 4-wheel drive road in the summer. Being a road, it's wide enough to walk side by side.

SOUTH SHORE/AMERICAN RIVER CANYON

Fully exposed, we welcomed the sun on this chilly late January afternoon. Turning around, the views of the Sierra unfolded. The ridges looked uninviting in some ways. Maybe that was because I know how much more work they are to climb compared to this little hill.

In the summer it's easy to hit both peaks – it's called Twin Peaks, after all. On the other side is the tower with the warning light for aircraft. From there is a view to Lake Tahoe Airport, Lake Tahoe Golf Course and Meyers. It takes a bit of bushwhacking through the manzanita in summer. That prospect sounded horrible on snowshoes. Instead, we sauntered up by the massive granite boulders to take in views of Lake Tahoe to our right. Angora Ridge, with her barren trees from the 2007 fire by the same name, was stark against the brilliant white snow. Mount Tallac hovered beyond.

This is 3 miles round trip.

Emerald Bay Campground: Silence, Beauty, Emptiness

Scenic: 6
Challenge: 3
Special note: Without snow, there is ample parking off the road.
Getting there: From South Lake Tahoe, take Highway 89 north. Once you go through all the hairpin turns and are about to reach the stretch where Cascade Lake is on the left and Emerald Bay is on the right, the campground is on the right.

While it would have been nice to be able to start a fire at the campsite to warm up a bit, it was even better having the entire campground to ourselves.

As we descended to the shore of Emerald Bay, we walked through a blizzard. Not everyone realized the bay was to our left as we snowshoed down; the visibility was that poor. Fresh snow was gradually accumulating on the already snow-laden picnic tables in Eagle Point Campground.

Trekking through this 100-spot campground on snowshoes is ideal. Seldom is anyone else there. The solitude and tranquility are abundant. It's the scenery that will give you pause and reason to take a camera.

Pines and cedar loom tall. Only the crunching of snowshoes can be heard.

Early on there was an opportunity to hook up with the Rubicon Trail. Instead we went to the right, the opposite direction. Mostly we followed the snow-covered road. At one point we meandered off to get a view of the water below. When we reached the bottom-most campsite, we broke trail to reach the bay. There, the water lapped against the rocks. Icicles had formed on some of the vegetation. On the far side of Lake Tahoe, blue sky peaked out. A couple boats braved the winter weather.

Looking around, it was easy to understand why in 1969 Emerald Bay was designated a National Natural Landmark. This campground is part of the larger Emerald Bay State Park, which includes the whole bay and Vikingsholm. The state acquired the land in 1953 from Placerville lumberman Harvey West for half the amount of its appraisal.

Mileage is going to be dependent on how much one meanders around the camping area and along the shore. It's about 1 mile straight down on the road.

High Meadow: Straight Up, Straight Down

Scenic: 5
Challenge: 6
Special note: Note your surroundings because signage is not great.
Getting there: From South Lake Tahoe, turn onto Al Tahoe Boulevard. Turn right on Pioneer Trail. Turn left on Remington Trail. (Sierra House Elementary School is on the corner.) Follow signs to the end and park. On the trail, veer up and to the right.

I had to catch my breath at one point as I felt the pull in my legs and lungs at the same time. "That's why it's called High Meadow," Rosemary said.

Although there was dirt on the route most exposed to the sun, it still seemed easier to hike with snowshoes than just boots. As we kept climbing, the snow got better for this winter activity. Large conifers loomed overhead, casting shadows on this gloriously sunny day. While the temperature was chilly to begin with, the exertion had us losing layers.

Different spurs could have you exploring the High Meadow trail system for days. Star Lake is about six miles one-way. High Meadow is about one mile below the lake. It's possible to make this a long or short snowshoe depending on when you turn around.

In summer 2010, the U.S. Forest Service turned the meadow into a construction zone in order to restore Cold Creek. The evidence is not visible to the untrained eye. What's left is a healthier environment.

On our trek we made it to an earlier manmade disturbance – power lines. Power Line Trail gets its name from all those overhead wires that run through the forest. A vista of sorts beckoned us before we reached our end point. The knoll provided panoramic views in all directions. Lake Tahoe almost looked small below the forest. The clearing we used as a turnaround point provided spectacular views looking west to Mount Tallac, Pyramid Peak and other ridgetops in Desolation Wilderness.

Although signs are clearly posted that snowmobiles are not allowed where we were, the visible tracks prove the sleds had been out. Those tracks always make snowshoeing and cross country skiing easier. With the trail wide enough for a vehicle in places, it allowed us to walk at least two across. This made it easier to hear each other over the crunching of the snow.

Grass Lake: An Easy Escape Atop Luther Pass

Scenic: 5
Challenge: 3
Special note: Make a mental note of where you parked.
Getting there: From South Lake Tahoe, go west on Highway 50. In Meyers, go left onto Highway 89. At the crest of Luther Pass, Grass Lake is on the right. There are several pullouts for parking.

Flat, scenic and free equals perfect snowshoe conditions. Grass Lake is serene much of the winter. Some days the powder is like sugar, so easy to walk through. Others had been there before us so we didn't have to break trail if we didn't want to.

Waterhouse Peak (9,497 feet) is the highest, nearest landmark. And while that may sound like it is towering, Luther Pass, where Grass Lake is, is at 7,740 feet.

When there isn't much snow at lake level, this is an ideal place to snowshoe or cross country ski. Plenty of dogs are often out getting exercise, too. When snow isn't on the ground this is a marshy area. It's not a true lake.

SOUTH SHORE/AMERICAN RIVER CANYON

Even though Highway 89 is so close, its activity is only noticeable if you want it to be. That may sound odd, but I'm a firm believer people have the capability to tune out most distractions. The din of traffic is one of them.

Ironically, the three of us welcomed that traffic when we were done. We had committed one of the bigger mistakes while playing in the woods. No one paid attention to our starting point. That meant when we got back to the road we didn't know which way to go.

Renee and I were on the road while Rosemary stayed on the snow, almost parallel to us. We got around a bend and as far as the eye could see were no parked vehicles, just another curve. We thought we should turn around and head toward Hope Valley.

Then the three of us were on the road. It was time to hitchhike. After Rosemary got in a vehicle with a couple, their son and their granddaughter (of course we didn't know that's who they were at that time, or that they were super helpful), I asked Renee if she had gotten the license plate number or knew the make of the vehicle. Neither of us had that information. We knew Rosemary had been correct, that we should have kept going toward Meyers, after the Good Samaritans stopped to tell us they were going to look for our vehicle in the other direction. It wasn't long before Rosemary came driving up in her SUV.

I share this story because combined, the three of us had lived on the South Shore for decades. We're experienced at outdoor play in all seasons. We're normally smart women. For some reason we weren't that day. It was a good reminder that communication is necessary, that it's essential to look in all directions when starting off, and to have a focal point to know what to look for when returning. We were never going to be in danger based on where we were that day, but that might not always be the case. We were lucky. This was an experience we could laugh about as we shook our heads in disbelief.

SOUTH SHORE/AMERICAN RIVER CANYON

Lake Tahoe Golf Course: Above Par Fun

Scenic: 5
Challenge: 2
Special note: Sometimes the restaurant/bar is open in the winter.
Getting there: From South Lake Tahoe, go west on Highway 50. The golf course is on the right before hitting the heart of Meyers.

Golf courses offer some of most wonderful snowshoeing opportunities. They are flat, scenic and go on for miles. While golfers might think the trees are close together, winter recreationists find these plots of land to be wide open.

Such is the case with Lake Tahoe Golf Course. This is an 18-hole course for much of the year. In winter a snowmobile concessionaire usually operates there. To the right of the clubhouse is the route to get away from the motorized fun. We started to the left of hole 10.

The noise from the motorized sleds dissipated quickly. The exhaust, though, was noticeable as we returned. It was clearly stinking up the fresh mountain air.

One of the nice things about this trek was that it didn't take long to reach a serene landscape. Plenty of people had been there before us. Snowshoe and cross country ski tracks crisscrossed each other. Some of the ski tracks were so worn it was as if they had been professionally laid.

The snow was perfect this particular day so breaking trail was no big deal, and in many ways was more fun. The give to the snow made it relatively easy to push through and a bit more of a workout than going where others had already gone.

A few bridges across the Upper Truckee River and Angora Creek have barriers to keep snowmobilers out. It means either having to gingerly step over them or taking off your equipment.

Many of the South Shore's more recognizable peaks made themselves known as we went farther: Freel, Jobs, Mount Tallac, and Twin Peaks next door.

The golf course sits on state land, namely Lake Valley State Recreation Area. It abuts Washoe Meadows State Park. There are several access points to both. The golf course provides the most parking, especially on days when parking on a street could be problematic because of snow removal.

Distance is all dependent on how far one goes.

West Shore

Sugar Pine Point State Park is a recreation playground.

Sugar Pine Point: Olympic History

Scenic: 5
Challenge: Varies
Special note: Dogs are not allowed. Trails are free, but it costs to park.
Getting there: From South Lake Tahoe, go north on Highway 89. Before hitting Tahoma, on the right will be a sign for the Ehrman Mansion. In less than one mile, make a left turn into the Sugar Pine Point Campground.

People with guns on cross country skis. That certainly set the tone for a unique day in the woods. Fortunately, they were shooting at electronic targets with laser rifles.

A sign saying "Olympic Heritage Event" made us wonder if we should turn around because we are nowhere near Olympic caliber athletes in any sport.

While snowshoeing is allowed at Sugar Pine Point State Park, the history here is rooted in the cross country skiing. This course was used for the 1960 Winter Olympics that were based at Squaw Valley. Now, competitions for non-Olympians are scheduled throughout the season, with biathlon events (where guns are used) part of the mix. Guided full moon snowshoe treks are offered on the lake side of the park.

At the shooting range, Holly Beatie was dispensing a wealth of information. She is well versed in the world of biathlon – which is the sport of cross country skiing and shooting. She moved to the North Shore of Lake Tahoe in the 1970s, but no women's biathlon teams existed so she competed with the men. It wasn't until 1980 that the U.S. developed a women's team. In 1984, Beatie was on the inaugural U.S. biathlon team at the Women's World Championships in Chamonix, France, which won the bronze.

We left the competitors behind to strike out on the myriad trails in this state park along Lake Tahoe's West Shore. Steeped in history, interpretive signs along the way pointed out facts about the 1960 Olympics. At the entrance is a sign called the Tower of Nations, which is similar to what spectators at the 1960 Olympics were welcomed with.

When snowshoeing or walking anywhere near groomed cross country tracks, stay out of them. This is basic etiquette in the snowsports world.

Fluorescent green lichen covered several trees. A few charred trees along the way were a reminder of the August 2007 Washoe Fire that destroyed five houses and burned about 15 acres. General Creek meanders between many of the trails, though it was not visible most of the time. However, at a few junctures we crossed it via a bridge.

Five distinct trails are listed as beginner, intermediate and beginner/intermediate. They range from 1.2 to 3.3 miles. Two are on the lake side; three on the west side of the highway. It's possible to do more than one. Grab a trail map at one of the park entrances.

East Shore

Skunk Harbor is awash in views starting at the beginning of the route.

Marlette Lake: Solitude Escape In Winter

Scenic: 7
Challenge: 8
Special note: Go early because of the shortened winter days.
Getting there: From South Lake Tahoe, take Highway 50 east. At the top of Spooner Summit, just beyond the Highway 28 junction, there is parking on the left. Trail starts there. Keep Spooner Lake to your left. The North Canyon Trail will eventually be on the right.

Sitting on the rocks I wished I were in a chair that spun around so I didn't have to get up to enjoy the 360-degree view of this slice of Sierra beauty.

On this particular day we had Marlette Lake to ourselves. In winter, this trail is practically deserted; the complete opposite of summer and fall when hikers and mountain bikers are out.

It was stunning, warm and relaxing, especially after trekking nearly 6 miles to get there. While we started out with the notion we would be snowshoeing, the hard pack conditions were such that hiking boots were all we needed for most of the trip. It was nice to have the snowshoes for the final descent to the lake, and then climbing out. Poles also made for easier trekking.

At times part of the trail will be groomed for cross country skiing. Snowmobilers will often lay down a path that makes shoeing/walking easier. Much of the trail is wide enough for at least two to walk side by side because this is North Canyon Road.

The bare aspens were like tall white, stick figures protruding from the snow.

Marlette's history is rich, dating back to the days when silver was mined in Nevada. The dam forming the lake was built in 1873. The height of it has been increased several times; it's now at 45 feet high. The lake is 45 feet deep.

While fishing at Marlette did not open until 2006, brook trout were introduced in the 1800s, Lahontan cutthroat trout in 1964, and rainbow trout in 1984.

The rock island where we stopped for lunch had a sign talking about some of the history, including the chimney that remains on Rocky Point. It's the last remnant of what was a cabin built by James Mather Leonard and Jessie Hobart Leonard in 1933. They owned Virginia City Water Company. Marlette Lake, which provides water to Virginia City, was part of the company's holdings. Before the couple built the cabin, the other area structures were a caretaker's cabin near the dam and a Nevada Fish and Game cabin. The caretaker's cabin was supposed to be taken down in the late 1960s, but instead crews mistakenly took down the Leonard cabin. In 2005, the chimney was restored. The informational sign was erected in 2014 on Jessie Leonard's 91st birthday.

The state bought the water system in 1963 from the Curtis Wright Corp., which had bought it from the Leonards. The Marlette Water System, which still provides water to Virginia City, Gold Hill, Silver City and part of Carson City, also includes Hobart Reservoir.

EAST SHORE

Skunk Harbor: Just The Name Stinks

Scenic: 7
Challenge: 5
Special note: All the work is on the return trip.
Getting there: From South Lake Tahoe, go east on Highway 50, up Spooner Summit. Turn left onto Highway 28. Parking is on the left in 2.4 miles. Nevada Department of Transportation clears the area so parking is not right on the highway.

Seclusion, mixed with vast views of Lake Tahoe is what the trek to Skunk Harbor is all about.

Sometimes there is no clear starting point because of all the snow. Some years it's a pretty steep first 15 feet before it flattens out. Fortunately, a snowmobiler had laid a track for us, as had other snowshoers and cross country skiers.

While I try not to go off a dirt trail for erosion reasons, with so much snow it was inviting at times to break trail, traipsing through the virgin white. Sometimes it was fluffy; other times it was crunchy.

No matter where one looked, it was a winter wonderland. It didn't take long for Lake Tahoe to come into view. The openness of the trail in many ways made me feel like I was much farther removed from civilization than I was.

Tracks led to a knoll that we scampered up to get what was a stunning view of much of the lake. It's unfortunate such a lovely place has such a smelly name.

If only it had been warmer. Warmth and snowshoeing in winter are often elusive. Lingering on the beach this time of year is much different than in summer – not so inviting. Ice hung from some of the rocks along the shore. About a foot-wide stretch of sand was exposed.

Remnants of Skunk Harbor's past were visible. While the U.S. Forest Service now owns this swath of land on the East Shore, that wasn't always the case. Stone buildings near the waterfront once belonged to George and Caroline Newhall. They used it as a second home for their San Francisco friends in the 1920s. George Whittell then became the land owner. He once owned most of the East Shore down to Zephyr Cove. Pilings for what once was a pier protrude from the water.

It's a gradual 1.5-mile descent from the highway to the beach. The uphill ascent doesn't feel so gradual. The elevation change is 560 feet.

Alpine County

The ruggedness of the Sierra can be found in Alpine County.

Elephants Back: Climb Aboard For The Scenery

Scenic: 8
Challenge: 7
Special note: A sno-park permit is required between Nov. 1-May 30. They may be purchased online.
Getting there: From South Lake Tahoe, go west on Highway 50. In Meyers, be in the left lane in the roundabout, taking the second exit onto Highway 89. At the T in Hope Valley, go right on Highway 88. At the top of Carson Pass, park on the left. The trailhead is by the Carson Ranger District building.

It was one of those incredibly perfect Sierra days: the sun beaming down, the sky a deep blue with streaks of white clouds, not even a wisp of wind at the top, surrounded by nature's beauty in the company of friends. If only these moments could be bottled.

This is how Craig and his six women – me, Sue, Donna, Suzy, Carolyn and Trish – started one New Year's Day; with a snowshoe to the top of Elephants Back in the Mokelumne Wilderness.

We took our time. Donna's gadget recorded us being in the wilderness for about four hours; only two of which actually involved walking. We put in 4.61 miles, gained 1,168 feet in elevation, and went to 9,584 feet. Photo stops were a necessity, as was a leisurely lunch at the top.

One reason for choosing this excursion was knowing there would be more snow here than at lake level. Plus, much of the trail is exposed so there was less likelihood of ice being an issue. The trail starts off narrow, which meant we were single file. The snow was hard in this section, so the claws on the snowshoes were welcome. So were the poles for a better sense of balance.

It didn't take long for Elephants Back and Round Top Peak to show themselves. At one point, Frog Lake was on our left and Woods Lake on our right in the distance. Part of this is also a segment of the Pacific Crest Trail.

Plenty of people had been here before us. While it's nice not to break trail, there were too many trails at times. We knew the direction we should be headed and had plenty of daylight, so it was no big deal. It might be a bit disorienting for those who are unfamiliar with the area.

Pausing, we turned around and not too far in the distance was Caples Lake. From this perspective it looked large and completely covered in ice.

At the base of Elephants Back the snow was like sugar. While it was ideal for our purposes, it would likely pose an avalanche danger once more snow arrived. This consistency does not make for a good base.

It was not until we were part way up Elephants Back that we were able to see a frozen Winnemucca Lake at the base of Round Top. We took off our snowshoes to make it up the loose volcanic rock of Elephants Back. There was no way to snowshoe to the top. That didn't matter. The views at the top of Elephants Back are some of the best to be had in such a short distance, especially since the expanse of beauty spills forth in every direction.

On our way out we saw people headed to Round Top with the intention of skiing down.

ALPINE COUNTY

Carson Pass: Ruggedness Mixed With Beauty

Scenic: 8
Challenge: 7
Special note: This requires at least two vehicles because it's a one-way trek.
Getting there: From South Lake Tahoe, head west on Highway 50. In Meyers, be in the left lane in the roundabout, taking the second exit onto Highway 89. At the T intersection, turn right onto Highway 88. Go past the parking area atop Carson Pass. Start at Meiss Trailhead, which is on the right. Leave a car at the Caltrans maintenance station farther down Highway 88.

For 360 degrees it was a winter wonderland. It was like being in the middle of the Sierra with mountains as far as the eye could see. Distinguishable landmarks dotted the landscape – Elephants Back, the runs at Kirkwood Mountain Resort, Little Round Top, Round Top, Hawkins Peak and others. Meiss Meadow resembled a frozen lake; with one person saying the cabins looked like Monopoly board pieces. Caples Lake, covered in ice and snow, was uninviting. The view of sapphire-colored Lake Tahoe may have been what General John Fremont saw when he first laid eyes on this alpine wonder.

What a glorious way to welcome in the new year.

Five of us spent a morning on an incredible snowshoe in the Carson Pass-Kirkwood cross country ski area. Plenty of tracks could be seen, presumably mostly from backcountry skiers. For the most part we were breaking trail. We knew where we wanted to go, but there was no set trail to get us there. That added to the fun.

It was minus 7 degrees in Meyers as we drove through. At the trail's starting point it was 10 degrees and had warmed to 22 by the time we were done. What a thermometer would have read on the ridge, where the wind howled to the point it seemed to take our breath away, well, it's probably better we didn't know.

That wind whipped ice formations onto rocks in what looked like works of art, especially with the orange lichen nearby. At times the snow was so hard our snowshoes made no indentation, while at other times it was like floating on pillow-like powder. In other spots it was a crusty layer we punched through.

From the trailhead we headed nearly straight up and then to the left toward the ridge we knew we wanted to trek along. Had we continued, Little Round Top would have added at least another three miles to our journey. We opted to drop down into a bowl. At the bottom we hooked up with the groomed trails of Kirkwood Cross Country and Snowshoe Center before we made our way to the Caltrans maintenance station where we had left a vehicle.

In all, we went 6.55 miles. We started at 8,573 feet and reached a maximum elevation of 9,444 feet. With the up and down route, we gained a total of 1,654 feet in elevation and descended 2,267 feet.

Hope Valley: 60 Miles Of Designated Trails

Scenic: 4
Challenge: 5
Special note: Make a donation for trail use when the yurt is up.
Getting there: From South Lake Tahoe, take Highway 50 west. In Meyers, be in the left lane in the roundabout, taking the second exit onto Highway 89. Go over Luther Pass. At the four-way stop go straight toward the yurt. Park.

Two things about steadily climbing up are often true: a great view is usually the first reward, and the trip down is often a breeze. Both are true on this snowshoe in Hope Valley. This is one of those areas just outside the Lake Tahoe Basin that is worth visiting year round.

With more than 60 miles of marked trails, it has a variety of terrain to satisfy all levels of snowshoers and cross country skiers. Added bonuses include free parking and no trail fee. However, Hope Valley Outdoors gladly takes donations. After all, it takes a tremendous amount of work to keep up this outdoor playground on the Humboldt-Toiyabe National Forest.

As we climbed, the forest seemed to hug us. We forgot there was a highway close by.

Although Burnside Road is drivable for a bit in the summer, in the winter no tires are allowed across the snow. We seemed to have this oasis to ourselves. It wasn't until we headed back that we finally came across other people out playing.

We followed the signs toward Secret Meadow, even though it meant going downhill. As we meandered around in a loop, openings peaked out to Hope Valley below us. Seeing the field of snow made me wonder what this meadow must look like in the spring and summer. Are there wildflowers? Is it grassy? Would it make for a great lunch spot? Is it as peaceful during hiking season as it is in snowshoeing season?

Continuing on a bit, a smile crossed my face. I saw a swing in the distance. I love to swing; that gentle rocking back and forth. With snowshoes on, it made for an interesting dismount.

We continued on, circling back to the main road. We kept going up. A sign pointed to a vista. The Carson Range seemed to go on forever. Stevens Peak loomed tallest from this vantage point. Maps and research are not consistent with its elevation – some say close to 10,000 feet, while others have it topping that mark. The peak is named after J.M. Stevens, who was a supervisor in Alpine County and ran a stagecoach in Hope Valley in the 1860s.

Sitting on the granite boulder having a bite to eat I took in the scenery. It's sad to see the blackened trees charred from the 2008 Burnside Fire.

Signs along the various trails are abundant, but not obnoxiously so. Maps are often available in the yurt just in case. Mileage will be dependent on your route. Lessons, tours and equipment rentals are also available when the yurt is open, with opening day usually on the Winter Solstice in December. Dogs are allowed, but no trash service exists, so pack everything out. This is a great place to snowshoe and cross country ski.

www.ingramcontent.com/pod-product-compliance
Lightning Source LLC
Chambersburg PA
CBHW030138100526
44592CB00011B/941